Mother Goose
on the Loose

Designer: Angela Carlino
Production Manager: Hope Koturo

Library of Congress Cataloging-in-Publication Data

Goldstein, Bobbye S.
  Mother Goose on the loose : cartoons from the New Yorker / by Bobbye S. Goldstein.
      p. cm.
Summary: A collection of Mother Goose rhymes and original nursery rhymes
based on familiar tales illustrated with cartoons from the New Yorker magazine.
  ISBN 0-8109-4239-9
  1. Nursery rhymes. 2. Children's poetry. [1. Nursery rhymes. 2. Cartoons and comics.] I. Title.
  PZ8.3.G5743 Mo 2003
  398.8—dc21

                                                          2002009802

Published in 2003 by Harry N. Abrams, Incorporated, New York

Printed and bound in Singapore
10 9 8 7 6 5 4 3 2 1

Harry N. Abrams, Inc.
100 Fifth Avenue
New York, N.Y. 10011
www.abramsbooks.com

Abrams is a subsidiary of LA MARTINIÈRE
                           G R O U P E

illustrated with cartoons from THE NEW YORKER

Mother Goose
on the Loose

edited by Bobbye S. Goldstein

HARRY N. ABRAMS, INC., PUBLISHERS

To my son Freddy
With love
—B.S.G.

Contents

Hey Diddle Diddle

Hey diddle diddle,
The cat and the fiddle,
The cow jumped over the moon;
The little dog laughed,
To see such sport,
And the dish ran away with the spoon.

"It's a cow thing. You wouldn't understand."

"Son, your mother is a remarkable woman."

"*I guess it's no big deal anymore.*"

"Let's say, God forbid, you <u>don't</u> make it over the moon.
We still make a killing with the merchandising thing."

"*Your insurance coverage allows for a lot of really foolhardy stunts, Madam,
but jumping over the moon, I'm afraid, is not one of them.*"

"*There should also be a little dog laughing to see such sport.*"

"Quick! Follow that dish and spoon!"

"When 'Hey Diddle Diddle' came along, we jumped at the chance to work together."

"Do we have your blessing?"

"*I myself don't see much hope for an inter-utensil relationship.*"

"We're raising the children as forks."

"Sometimes I'm sorry I ever ran away with you."

"Perhaps if you weren't paying so much alimony we could eat out once in a while."

Hickory, Dickory, Dock

Hickory, dickory, dock,
The mouse ran up the clock.
The clock struck one,
The mouse ran down,
Hickory, dickory, dock.

"What did you think of 'Hickory, Dickory, Dock'?"

Little Bo-Peep

Little Bo-Peep has lost her sheep,
And doesn't know where to find them;
Leave them alone, and they'll come home,
Wagging their tails behind them.

"*As I call each of your names, please answer by saying 'present.'*"

Jack and Jill

Jack and Jill
Went up the hill,
To fetch a pail of water;
Jack fell down,
And broke his crown
And Jill came tumbling after.

"Jack, when we get down the hill, let's put the pail up for auction."

Little Jack Horner

Little Jack Horner
Sat in the corner,
Eating a holiday pie;
He put in his thumb,
And pulled out a plum,
And said, "What a good boy am I!"

"So, when he says, 'What a good boy am I,' Jack is really reinforcing his self-esteem."

Mary Had a Little Lamb

Mary had a little lamb,
Whose fleece was white as snow;
And everywhere that Mary went
The lamb was sure to go.

"*Mary had a little lamb, whose fleece was white as snow....*"

Old Mother Hubbard and Her Dog

Old Mother Hubbard
Went to the cupboard,
To fetch her poor dog a bone;
But when she got there
The cupboard was bare
And so the poor dog had none.

"I'm afraid the cupboard is bare again, Mrs. Hubbard."

Goldilocks and the Three Bears

What Goldilocks did
Was really not right,
Leaving the bears' house
A miserable sight.
—B.S.G.

*"We are in the bears' house. Goldilocks has just eaten
a bowl of porridge. Papa Bear enters."*

"They're offering a deal—you pay court costs and damages,
they drop charges of breaking and entering."

"Hey, Al, we have anything in matched sets that's not too
hard and not too soft but just right?"

Pease Porridge

Pease porridge hot,
Pease porridge cold,
Pease porridge in the pot,
Nine days old.
Some like it hot,
Some like it cold,
Some like it in the pot
Nine days old.

"Oh, don't mind us, we're just gathering peas for our porridge."

Old King Cole

Old King Cole was a merry old soul,
And a merry old soul was he;
He called for his pipe,
And he called for his bowl,
And he called for his fiddlers three.

"Hah! <u>This</u> is the Old King Cole nobody ever sees."

"No more pipe, and no more bowl."

"Call my accountants three."

Humpty Dumpty

Humpty Dumpty sat on a wall,
Humpty Dumpty had a great fall;
All the King's horses and all the King's men,
Couldn't put Humpty together again.

"Humpty Dumpty sat on a wall, Humpty Dumpty had a great fall.
Details at eleven on your local news."

"You might want to sit down, Mrs. Dumpty."

"I'm afraid you have only three minutes to live."

"If a fall doesn't kill you, your high cholesterol level will."

"It's okay. I'm hard-boiled."

"*This may not be your fault.*"

"He's in an H.M.O. Get some of the King's horses and a few of the King's men."

"Gentlemen, the fact that all my horses and all my men couldn't put Humpty together again simply proves to me that I must have <u>more</u> horses and <u>more</u> men."

"Maybe they didn't try hard enough."

This Little Piggy

This little piggy went to market,
This little piggy stayed home,
This little piggy had roast beef,
This little piggy had none,
And this little piggy cried,
"Wee, wee, wee"
All the way home.

"Oh, Miss Finnegan, which little piggy was it had roast beef?"

Three Blind Mice

Three blind mice, see how they run!
They all ran after the farmer's wife,
Who cut off their tails with a carving knife,
Did you ever see such a thing in your life,
As three blind mice?

"She cut off his <u>what</u> with a carving knife?"

Jack and the Beanstalk

When Jack climbed up the beanstalk
A mean giant he did meet,
So Jack slid down the beanstalk
And made a fast retreat!

—B.S.G.

"Burpee wasn't kidding."

JACK AND THE GIANT VEGETARIAN

" '*Then Jack traded his cow for five magic beans.*' *Here's a copy*
of the contract, the accounting summary, the insurance waiver, the
shareholders' briefing, and the receipt."

"We're pleased to announce that your company has shrewdly traded a cow for some magic beans."

Peter Piper

Peter Piper picked a peck of pickled peppers;
A peck of pickled peppers Peter Piper picked.
If Peter Piper picked a peck of pickled peppers,
Where's the peck of pickled peppers Peter Piper picked?

"Dear Diary: Today I picked a peck of pickled peppers."

Rich Man, Poor Man

Rich man
Poor man
Beggar man
Thief
Doctor
Lawyer
Indian Chief

Rock-A-Bye-Baby

Rock-a-bye-baby
On the tree top,
When the wind blows
The cradle will rock.
When the bough breaks,
The cradle will fall,
And down will come baby,
Cradle and all.

*"Rock-a-bye-baby
on the tree top,
When the wind blows
the cradle will rock . . ."*

Sing a Song of Sixpence

Sing a song of sixpence,
A pocket full of rye;
Four and twenty blackbirds,
Baked in a pie.
When the pie was opened,
The birds began to sing;
Wasn't that a dainty dish,
To set before a king?

"Contains four and twenty dolphin-free,
blackbird flavored whitefish pieces."

The Crooked Man

There was a crooked man,
And he walked a crooked mile,
He found a crooked sixpence
Against a crooked stile;
He bought a crooked cat
Which caught a crooked mouse,
And they all lived together
In a little crooked house.

"There was a crooked man!
He walked a crooked mile!
Then he gradually improved his posture
with corrective massage techniques
and realignment therapy!"

The Old Woman in a Shoe

There was an old woman
Who lived in a shoe,
She had so many children
She didn't know what to do;
She gave them some broth
Without any bread;
She whipped them all soundly
And sent them to bed.

"No, I didn't call a taxi."

"The old shoe hasn't been the same since the kids grew up."

"Yes, I can remember when it was nothing but forest land as far as you could see."

"Now that the children are gone, I'm leasing twenty-seven hundred square feet for immediate occupancy, warehousing several luxury units, and aiming for complete co-op conversion by early September."

The Owl and the Pussy-Cat

The Owl and the Pussy-Cat went to sea
In a beautiful pea-green boat;
They took some honey and plenty of money,
Wrapped up in a five-pound note.

—Edward Lear

"I'll try to be more like the owl if you'll be more like the pussycat."

Little Red Riding Hood

Little Red Riding Hood
On that fateful day
Was out to help Grandma
Not just to play!

—B.S.G.

"Your grandma and I have decided to live together."

"It's too hot to eat."

"*My, Grandma, what a big-shot attorney you have.*"

"*And all this time I didn't think you'd understand
why I ate your grandma and took her place.*"

*"Wow, dearie, did you miss the action! A wolf was bugging me, so I gave
him a shot of Mace, karated him, and called the fuzz."*

"Gosh, Grandma, what a big office you have!"

Little Red Riding Hood 89

Star Light

Star light, star bright,
First star I see tonight,
I wish I may, I wish I might,
Have the wish I wish tonight.

"Star light, star bright, first star I see . . . "

Old Mother Goose and the Golden Egg

Old Mother Goose,
When she wanted to wander,
Would ride through the air
On a very fine gander.

Mother Goose had a house,
'Twas build in a wood,
Where an owl at the door
For sentinel stood.

She had a son Jack,
A plain-looking lad,
He was not very good,
Nor yet very bad.

She sent him to market,
A live goose he bought,
"See, mother," says he,
"I have not been for nought."

Jack's goose and her gander
Grew very fond;
They'd both eat together,
Or swim in the pond.

Jack found one fine morning,
As I have been told,
His goose had laid him
An egg of pure gold.

"Just once, before I die, I'd like to lay a golden egg."

"*The Goose That Lays the Golden Eggs is proud to announce she's now laying two additional lines of eggs; Silver and Platinum.*"

The Three Little Pigs

The three little pigs
Had quite a scare,
When the big bad wolf
Came calling there.

—B.S.G.

"*Once upon a time there were these three little pigs. There was a neurotic little pig, a psychotic little pig, and a normal little pig . . . .*"

*"The little pig with the portfolio of straw and the little pig
with the portfolio of sticks were swallowed up, but the
little pig with the portfolio of bricks withstood the dip in the market."*

From the Desk of Mother Goose
Memo: Spread the Word!

Enjoy these cartoons
And these rhymes
And read them over
Many times!
    —M. Goose

Afterword

Where did you get the idea? How did you get started with this book? These are the questions I've been asked ever since I began the pleasurable journey of uniting Mother Goose rhymes and a few classic children's stories with relevant cartoons from *The New Yorker*.

From childhood on I was always a reader. The lure of the printed word was my favorite pastime. When I was a young child, my family lived next door to the public library. People used to tease me and say that proximity was part of the reason for my fascination with books and reading. My parents believed in nurturing my sisters and me with poetry, books, and music, and we grew up happily in that atmosphere and environment.

When my young son who is now grown, and to whom this book is dedicated, started school, the hot topics were comic books and television and their influence on reading and writing. The Parents' Council at his school asked me to do a presentation on cartoons and comics in relation to early childhood education. In doing research for that presentation, I learned a great deal about the subject.

Cartoons, comic strips, bumper stickers, headlines, and haiku are a few of the concise ways to bring a message to the public. A cartoon is generally a one-frame picture, whereas comic strips usually have a series of frames. A cartoon conveys one idea, often of a satirical nature. Comic strips tell a story, sometimes a continuing story. Both cartoons and comic strips have universal appeal, and some wordless cartoons are syndicated worldwide.

Originally some educators felt that only simple words could be used in cartoons and comics. Therefore, they could not be a meaningful or helpful tool in the instruction of reading. However, while a reading specialist in District 3, Manhattan, New York City, I conducted a year's research study on using cartoons and comic strips in teaching reading. We found that cartoons frequently used complex words and expressions to present a theme. This helped expand the participants' vocabulary and comprehension. In an interesting aside, the children who were involved in the study began drawing their own cartoons, modeling them on basic facts that they had learned. The results of my study were published in an article, "Looking at cartoons and comics in a new way," in the *Journal of Reading* (v. 29, no. 7, 4/86) of the International Reading Association, of which I am a former board member.

For over two hundred years, comics and cartoons have appeared in American newspapers and magazines, eventually becoming a regular feature. Many newspapers today have resident cartoonists who supply timely political cartoons on a daily basis. Others rely on freelance artists and call upon them to depict current problems and situations.

Benjamin Franklin is hailed as the first political cartoonist in America. He published the famous "Join or Die" drawing when he proposed a plan of union for the Colonies. The cartoon first appeared in 1754, then again in 1765 and 1776.

Some cartoons and comic strips are for entertainment and enjoyment, while editorial cartoons, usually found on the editorial pages of a newspaper, inform and highlight current controversies. They can influence public opinion. Boss Tweed, a New York City politician (1823–1878), said, "I don't care a straw for your news paper articles, my constituents don't know how to read, but they can't help seeing them *#@! pictures." These were his comments about the anti–Boss Tweed political cartoons of Thomas Nast, a cartoonist at that time.

Over the years several prominent museums have had exhibitions of cartoons and comics. Among them, the Museum of Modern Art, New York, honored Mickey Mouse in 1978 and showed how he evolved from a rambunctious mouse into a lovable, international icon. Subsequently, in 1992 the museum had a special exhibit of cartoon artist Art Spiegelman's work. In 1995, the Library of Congress held an exhibit "Featuring the Funnies: 100 Years of Comic Strips." The show was scheduled to coincide with the 100th anniversary of the appearance of the first comic strip in a New York newspaper, *The New York World.* To commemorate the celebration, the United States Postal Service issued special cartoon stamps.

There are many beautiful traditional Mother Goose books on the market today with outstanding illustrations. My personal dream was to bring a new approach to Mother Goose in the twenty-first century by relating the timeless and timely rhymes and tales of yesterday–many born as social and political, often satirical, commentary of their day–with today's events, as reflected in the cartoons of *The New Yorker.* Uniting these two genres results in an interesting and entertaining combination for all readers, young and old. This format may be used as a springboard for social and political discussions, supplemented with contemporary cartoons from local newspapers. Also the book encourages discussion of points of view, irony, and satire.

While looking for the Mother Goose cartoons, I also found a number of ones related to popular children's stories, such as "Goldilocks and the Three Bears" and "Little Red Riding Hood." There were too few of these cartoons to compile a second volume, but it seemed a shame not to include them. Reproducing the text of the stories in full, however, would have overwhelmed the project and detracted from the cartoons. Upon the encouragement of my editor, I wrote simple verses in the nursery rhyme tradition to accompany the cartoons inspired by the tales.

With thanks to the talented cartoonists at *The New Yorker,* the people at The Cartoon Bank, and my publisher Harry N. Abrams, Inc., my dream has come true.

Bobbye S. Goldstein

Acknowledgments

I am pleased to recognize those who helped me on the path from idea to publication.

The manuscript was first sent to Jonathan Schmidt, a caring colleague, who forwarded it to his friend at Abrams, my terrific editor, Howard Reeves. Emily Farbman and Linas Alsenas were Howard's capable assistants. I also wish to thank Jane Cavolina, who enthusiastically shared my vision and acted as my liaison with Bob Mankoff.

A highlight in my life was actually meeting the personable and multi-talented Bob Mankoff, cartoon editor of *The New Yorker* as well as founder and president of The Cartoon Bank, who helped me to obtain permission to use *The New Yorker* cartoons. I also wish to thank Andy Pillsbury and Bodin Suttles, both of The Cartoon Bank, for their exacting detail and assistance throughout the project.

Always there for me, with her wonderful listening ear, and great way with words, was my dear sister Shirley Frances Flax.

Frederic S. Goldstein, my caring and considerate son, graciously and superbly assisted me in so many ways, despite his own busy career. In addition, he used his extensive computer expertise to facilitate the organization and compilation of this book. (To the next generation, his children, my grandchildren, Jeffrey and Emily, enjoy the traditional rhymes and accompanying cartoons!)

During the time we were working on this book, three treasured and cherished loved ones passed away: my beloved husband, Dr. Gabriel F. Goldstein; my devoted sister, Eleanor R. Schwartz Pearl; and Bob Mankoff's dear mother, Mollie Mankoff. I also dedicate this book in their memory.

Bobbye S. Goldstein

"It goes, 'Hickory dickory dock' and then a damn mouse runs up it."

Index of Illustrators